Feeling Waves

A Collection of Haiku

By
Elijah 'Goose' Kazlauskas

AOS Publishing, 2025

ISBN: 978-1-998662-78-4

Cover Design: Meredith Lindsay

Visit AOS Publishing's website:
www.aospublishing.com

Dedicated to Jennifer Button

ACKNOWLEDGEMENTS

An earlier version of Feeling Waves Haiku #1 was previously published in Dreamers Magazine Issue 12.

Feeling Waves Haiku #12 was previously published in Wingless Dreamer's anthology, Erotica of Eternity, as One Haiku.

1

Snow falls into rain
since I lost all but eight words
that my first love gave.

2

You deserved fifteen
years' worth of lifeline letters
instead of just one.

3

Merciless time eats
at names surrounded by hearts
carved on trees with love.

4

Traffic lights reflect
on a river of rainfall.
We wait together.

5

The forgotten bell
chimes—I pass through frigid shards
of stained winter glass.

6

A lotus persists
in the violent river,
losing one petal.

7

Tears— "I'm out!" I run.
Turmoil has taken the night.
Loyalty saves me.

8

Others cheer up front.
Darkened, we watch from the back,
stifling our hatred.

9

As lights start to drift,
fear makes me tell you a lie:
I say not to wait.

10

I won't show my pain;
it's how I chase yours away.
"One bottle's enough."

11

Digging and yearning,
the falling rain is our song.
Growing takes patience.

12

All the seams have torn.
The night is no longer dark.
It's hard to breathe now.

13

A faint wind moves leaves.
One night might last forever.
Can we just be us?

14

There's shallow water
by all the poison barbs, thorns,
and golden petals.

15

These wings remind me
of my youth spent flying through
the endless, blue sky.

16

The field is cold now.
Snowflakes settle on a bird;
the rest have gone south.

17

The first day of spring:
even though it's still raining,
you walk in the sun.

18

Wishes pass throughout
this ephemeral, endless
moment—shall we dance?

19

The merry-go-round
at my back, waves crash ahead.
Freedom can't be far.

20

Eyes shutting, I trade
one darkness for another.
Fear is constricting.

21

Blooming in the night,
your face lulls me to a dream.
Let's count poppy seeds.

22

Your mouth promised me
candlelight in a dark storm
and red currant wine.

23

The sundial stopped;
our noses were side by side.
Seagulls sang to waves.

24

The icy pond's snow
is marred by countless footprints
until more snow falls.

25

Laughing, smiling eyes
with the light of a night sky...
just stopped opening.

26

It wasn't enough.
Many tried to grasp its wings,
but fell, abandoned.

27

The last time we drank,
she chased after a raccoon.
Soon the leaves will change.

28

Summer is over.
The flowers have all withered.
You forgot me, too?

29

The waves and the wind,
the singing and the drum's beat,
they led to dancing.

30

Snow White was poisoned.
Sleeping in her glass coffin,
she'll wait forever.

31

Friends, fire, waves, and
forgotten constellations.
We're hoping for love.

32

Sun glitter, resting;
you're here, a part of the view.
Red leaves start to fall.

33

My last dream brought me
back to your transient, gentle,
rosy cajoling.

34

How I miss seeing
the sun glitter-embraced waves
that surrounded us.

35

When I see the dock,
old memories cross my heart;
she used to stand there.

36

I hoped to find you
in the canopy of trees.
There were deer instead.

37

Heartbeats swayed from dreams.
Time swung precariously.
You kissed me goodbye.

38

The shrouded witch sighs.
Holding me, she promises,
"I'll come back again."

39

We'll never find it;
the fairy tales aren't real.
The clock struck midnight.

40

We saw Hollywood
then sent bottled messages,
but we still drifted.

41

The princesses dance
at a Halloween party.
I'm invisible.

42

Sitting by the cliff,
she reads, turning many pages
as the sun descends.

43

See that mermaid dance?
She's stepping on knives for love,
smiling away pain.

44

Fortune favours me.
The double vision moon lights
my way up the wheel.

45

She wore glass slippers.
How was her hair so golden?
Damn, what was her name?

46

Those Christmas winters
filled with sweet white violets
were the best of times.

47

Ocean waves shifting—
fantasies are good enough
for princes like me.

48

Wearing her white dress,
she waits in the cool twilight
for a memory.

49

"Do you ever just
want to cry all of the time?"
My long-held tears fall.

50

Her lovely dark eyes
shimmer like a city's lake
on a cloudy night.

51

It's dead on Mondays.
At the front of concession,
they hold hands and dance.

52

Every day, she's there.
Time and death keep us apart.
We should be in love.

53

Flurries fell that night.
My cold hand shook your warm one.
Will we meet again?

54

Glancing eyes will see
us together on the isle,
and yet we're not real.

55

Tears, laughter, and warm
feelings were exchanged in an
icy parking lot.

56

The remains of mechs
fill our once-beautiful world.
The Earth drank our blood.

57

The sunless tundra
made me used to loneliness,
but now I need help.

58

All of the trees here
want many sacrifices.
Don't stop your praying.

59

In your dream, you saw
a fire within a flood,
then awoke to rain.

60

Struggling through this swamp
makes me want to end it all,
and that frightens me.

61

The coiled chains bind me
beneath the rain. I pray for
a double rainbow.

62

Did you read it for
spontaneous combustion?
Was it worth your time?

63

Many clouds drift through
an eternal blue towards
autumn's horizon.

64

Hear it stalking you—
this jungle is draped in death;
you feel it watching.

65

The cacophonous
clouds approach; I don't want to
be forsaken here.

66

After much paddling,
we gladly fall asleep to
a loon's lullaby.

67

The words on the page
are lit by the glow of the
fragrant Christmas tree.

68

This island is ours.
Its ambient lights give way
to encouragement.

69

A rhyming breeze blows
down the beach, making her hair
dance around her face.

70

Through the barbed wire fence,
she would give her man flowers.
He made a mistake.

71

Boats sailed by and gulls
squawked merrily on the day
you first said hello.

72

We paddle with joy
on the wavy, midnight blue,
cherishing friendship.

73

Vibrant rainbow lights.
Bees visiting acacia.
Raindrops on water.

74

Keeping careful watch,
night waves kiss the starlit shore
as friends splash about.

75

The first winter's snow
and chiming church bells evoke
countless future dreams.

76

Love is moonlight, wind,
sunshine in the dead of night...
floodwaters as well.

77

The bond is severed.
We're over in October.
There are no regrets.

78

Pain shouldn't faze me.
I've fought every jungle beast,
so why does it hurt?

79

In the wilderness,
treasure is more plentiful.
See, X marks the spot.

80

How long have we been
stuck in lighting position?
This is endurance.

81

Grant restoration.
Find me in the tranquil light
when you turn the key.

82

The violets cry
out to the sky's dimming sun,
"You never loved me."

83

This is a prison.
Feel the chain of a closed door
wrap around your waist.

84

Sun-circled dark clouds
beckon us into the wind.
We're strong together.

85

The lock is broken.
Vengeance is mine to repay;
justice can see you.

86

"Drink a saccharin,
poisonous brew," said the witch.
"Leave this world behind."

87

Don't relive kisses
while struggling to free bound wrists.
Time shines through a prism.

88

The spell has been cast
and death's mistake corrected,
but you're not the same.

89

The panopticon
revelation is unknown
to the prisoners.

90

Faces on the wall,
proudly howling at the night,
for blood has been shed.

91

Pyramids stand tall.
Exodus cannot be seen.
Blood mixes with sand.

92

Ghosts, vamps, ghouls, and wolves
attend the underground rave,
searching for victims.

93

It's hard to be true;
the lion's den grips our hands,
but wings let us fly.

94

Among friends, nights spent
observing a dying world
are grim and glowing.

95

Where can you find love?
Locked deep inside a closed room:
a big mystery.

96

What do you dream of?
Are you flying with the stars?
Am I there with you?

97

Will I ever share
a morning's breakfast with you?
Round and round it goes.

98

Those were memories
made in my heart, a mirror
of warped reflections.

99

We still danced despite
not knowing the many steps.
We're always like that.

100

Amidst ice and snow,
another me, scared to dream,
is reflected here.

101

Never given hearts,
the familiars don't care
if they live or die.

102

Forgetting it all
would open the magic gate,
but who could forget?

103

The past is better
seen through a kaleidoscope
than through dark hatred.

104

A film's sad ending
makes me laugh at my own life.
It's not quite so bad.

105

Young platonic love
lies alongside passing time.
We lost many friends.

106

Skating on heart shards,
promising to watch ashes
while hunting for ghosts.

107

It's your birthday now.
You're so pretty in the glass,
dreaming mysteries.

108

Reflections cut too
deep in your flesh, you cry out
for an illusion.

109

The puzzle pieces
you don't put back together
still form a picture

110

Looking back, I stopped
to watch us become tragic.
Curtains always fall.

111

Our words contain love.
Sand flows through an old hourglass;
we are of one blood.

112

Lovers sharing space
often find themselves gazing
at each other's souls.

113

Knowing you are close,
I absorb myself in art
as clouds start to weep.

114

You promised me once
that I would die in your arms.
Why aren't you here now?

115

Raindrops fall lightly,
and my piano responds
with an honest song.

116

Silence surrounds us,
and I find your true feelings,
scattered in pages.

117

Arbitrarily,
I spy you glancing at me
with loving fondness.

118

Soothing rain can drown,
soft wind becomes violent,
snow's beauty is cold.

119

Though death claws away
at my life, I continue
to play to triumph.

120

Suddenly, an owl
lands next to your cage, hooting.
The bars fade to dust.

121

The sickness gets worse.
Always tending to my needs,
your passion has waned.

122

The hourglass shatters:
sand is blown away by wind,
but glass shards remain.

123

The rain grows in strength.
Even in your darkest dress,
you're a shooting star.

124

This dragon we've fed
needs to be killed before dawn
without last regrets.

125

Jumping off the cliff,
I embrace you in the air.
Gravity slows down.

126

She takes me around,
left, right, centre, up, and down,
through spaces of time.

127

Exit the roses,
walk the broken, twisted street,
while watching for glass.

128

She leaves at midnight.
Holding her coat, I follow.
We go to her place.

129

The ivory ice
stretches out towards countless
red, spiral towers.

130

Her cold pewter skin,
her rainbow gasoline eyes—
she's more than human.

131

Silken, crystal dreams
move through solid fantasies
into confusion.

132

Have you ever heard
such a pitiful, heartfelt,
melodeon song?

133

The gondola rides
on golden, starry, new waves
to someplace dreamed up.

134

Traces of your touch
remain on the marigolds.
The tears are gone, though.

135

Rhythm strikes a chord.
Can't you hear the tambourine?
Your second fiddle.

136

The dim, fiery light
of sunset covers the beach.
It wanes steadily.

137

Being enveloped
by a nostalgic perfume
is a friendly pain.

138

A dark corridor.
Candlelight travels down it.
A painting is lit.

139

We talk happily
while swinging at a slow pace
to dry ourselves off.

140

Every night, she calls.
If she stopped, would you feel it?
Or would you just sleep?

141

The midsummer moon
eclipses into a smile.
Open eyes are closed.

142

Galloping shadows
vie for a spot in the light.
They'll soon take over.

143

The spring sun rises.
Should love dream to stay awake?
My eyes meet your eyes.

144

Strolling through orchids,
your euphonious laughter
beckons a cool wind.

145

The feel of summer:
a dream come true is always
waiting within reach.

146

Quiet forgiveness.
Waves crash against vivid sand.
We leave our footprints.

147

The birds are flying
throughout the silver, champagne,
effervescent sky.

148

A winding river
underneath the time we shared
continues to flow.

149

The dusk horizon
reaches out desperately
through a herd of clouds.

150

Off the rocks we go,
into the cool, opaque waves.
We swim back to land.